ULTIMATE MANGA

HOW TO DRAW
MANGA
ADVENTURE

Marc Powell and David Neal

PowerKiDS press.

New York

WITH THANKS TO ODA, STEVE, AILIN, AND PAT

Published in 2016 by **The Rosen Publishing Group**
29 East 21st Street, New York, NY 10010

Copyright © 2016 Arcturus Holdings Limited

Text by Jack Hawkins
Edited by Jack Hawkins
Designed by Dynamo Ltd and Emma Randall
Cover design by Notion Design
Illustrations by Marc Powell and David Neal

Cataloging-in-Publication Data
Powell, Marc.
How to draw manga adventure / by Marc Powell and David Neal.
p. cm. — (Ultimate manga)
Includes index.
ISBN 978-1-4994-1144-7 (pbk.)
ISBN 978-1-4994-1153-9 (6 pack)
ISBN 978-1-4994-1180-5 (library binding)
1. Comic books, strips, etc. — Japan — Technique —
Juvenile literature. 2. Cartooning — Technique — Juvenile literature.
3. Comic strip characters — Japan — Juvenile literature. I. Title.
NC1764.5.J3 P694 2016
741.5'1—d23

Manufactured in the United States of America
CPSIA Compliance Information: Batch WS15PK: For Further Information
contact Rosen Publishing, New York, New York at 1-800-237-9932

CONTENTS

HOW TO USE THIS BOOK

The drawings in this book have been built up in seven stages. Each stage uses lines of a different color so you can see the new layer clearly. Of course, you don't have to use different colors in your work. Use a pencil for the first four stages so you can get your drawing right before moving on to the inking and coloring stages.

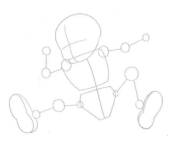

Stage 1: Green lines
This is the basic stick figure of your character.

Stage 2: Red lines
The next step is to flesh out the simple stick figure.

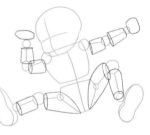

Stage 3: Blue lines
Then finish the basic shape and add in extra details.

Stage 4: Black lines
Add in clothes and any accessories.

Stage 5: Inks
The inking stage will give you a final line drawing.

Stage 6: Colors
"Flat" coloring uses lighter shades to set the base colors of your character.

Stage 7: Shading
Add shadows for light sources, and use darker colors to add depth to your character.

BASIC TOOLS

You don't need lots of complicated, expensive tools for your manga images – many of them are available from a good stationery shop. The others can be found in any art supplies store, or online.

PENCILS

These are probably the most important tool for any artist. It's important to find a type of pencil you are comfortable with, since you will be spending a lot of time using it.

Graphite

You will be accustomed to using graphite pencils – they are the familiar wood-encased "lead" pencils. They are available in a variety of densities from the softest, 9B, right up to the hardest, 9H. Hard pencils last longer and are less likely to smudge on the paper. Most artists use an HB (#2) pencil, which falls in the middle of the density scale.

Mechanical pencils

Also known as propelling pencils, these contain a length of lead that can be replaced. The leads are available in the same densities as graphite pencils. The great advantage of mechanical pencils over graphite is that you never have to sharpen them – you simply extend more lead as it wears down.

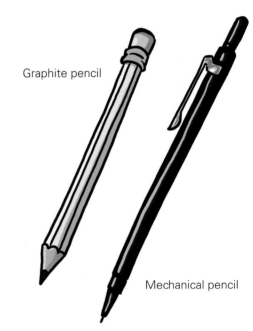

Graphite pencil

Mechanical pencil

Marker

Ballpoint pen

INKING PENS

After you have penciled your piece of artwork, you will need to ink the line to give a sharp, solid image.

Ballpoint pens

Standard ballpoint pens are ideal for lining your piece. However, their quality varies, as does their delivery of ink. A single good-quality ballpoint pen is better than a collection of cheap ones.

Marker pens

Standard marker pens of varying thicknesses are ideal for coloring and shading your artworks. They provide a steady, consistent supply of ink, and can be used to build layers of color by re-inking the same area. They are the tools most frequently used for manga coloring.

CLASSIC ANTIHERO

Most manga adventures are about heroes, but stories about antiheroes can be even more fun. Antiheroes have a selfish or rebellious streak. Here is a rough, rugged character with a steely gaze. Will he ever be able to work as part of a team?

STEP 1
Draw a basic stick figure with right arm raised and right leg in front of his left.

STEP 2
Use cylinder shapes to give bulk to your character's arms and legs, then draw the lines marking his neck and the basic shapes for his hands.

STEP 3

Draw the muscles in the arms, legs and torso and add the basic facial features. Now draw the hands and the handgun. The fingers and thumb of his left hand should be wrapped around the gun's grip.

STEP 4

Add details to the hands and facial features and give your character some hair. Now it's time to draw his clothes and ammunition belt.

STEP 5

Put the final touches to the antihero's clothing and give him some ammunition and facial hair. Use your lining pen to go over the lines that will be visible in the finished drawing and erase any pencil lines.

STEP 6
Using lighter shades, color in
your character. Drab tones give
him an air of menace.

STEP 7

Use shading to give depth to your character. Bear in mind the direction of the light when you are drawing the shadows.

● ARTIST'S TIP

Remember to make the outline thicker on items that are closer to the viewer. This helps to create depth in your character.

SASSY HEROINE

Characters in manga should never be taken at face value. This heroine might look friendly, but she has all the martial arts skills she needs to take on the meanest villains. Watch out for her whirlwind of fists and feet!

STEP 1

Draw a basic stick figure in a running pose, with her right foot raised and the knee crossing her left leg. Her left arm is foreshortened, as her elbow is pulled back. Female characters have rounder heads and pointier chins than males.

STEP 2

Expand the stick figure's arms, legs, and neck using cylinder shapes to give form to your character. Draw the basic shapes for her hands.

STEP 3
Add the anatomical details to her arms, legs and torso. Draw her fingers and basic facial features, including her extra-large eyes.

STEP 4
Next, give your character some hair and draw her dress, boots, and choker, taking care to show the gathers in her full skirt.

STEP 5
Add the final details to your heroine's clothes and use your lining pen to go over the lines that will be visible in the finished drawing. Erase any pencil lines.

STEP 6
Navy and white are the traditional colors for her sailor-style dress. Color in your character using lighter colors.

STEP 7

Use darker colors for shading to give depth to your figure. When you are drawing the shadows, bear in mind that the light is coming from her right-hand side.

ADVENTURE STORIES

Adventure manga can be a fast and frantic genre. Here are a few handy tips to help give your art more impact.

Action panel to panel

Because you are working with a pen and paper, keeping your action moving and your reader interested from panel to panel is key. In this simple, four-panel strip we show how you can make your adventure flow from panel to panel.

PANEL 1

It is important to suggest the atmosphere of your location in your first panel. This is obviously a large, enclosed forest, but the shadow in the foreground lets the viewer know that something sinister is lurking there.

PANEL 2

Hinting at danger has more effect than showing it right away. Here you can see that something is happening outside the panel and our hero knows danger is approaching.

PANEL 3
Now you can really kick the adventure up a notch by using focus lines and playing with perspective to create the dynamism of this T. rex crashing through the trees after your hero.

PANEL 4
Once the main action is reached, the background detail can be reduced to a minimum. You established the location in your previous panels so now you can focus purely on the action.

TAKEN TO THE LIMIT

Characters in adventure stories often have larger-than-life personalities. This can be used to your advantage, especially when drawing villains. Exaggerating the characteristics of your bad guys helps you to show their evil side. Play around with different techniques to show your villains at their worst.

Ordinary pirate
Here is a realistic approach to a manga pirate – scary and sinister. He could do with a little extra something – but what? Let's see . . .

Pirate extraordinaire
The character leaps into life when illustrated in a cartoon style. This approach allows you to show him in more exaggerated and dynamic poses.

ARMY GENERAL

We have given this mature military man a solid, strong body shape. For male characters you don't have to resort to rippling muscles on every part of the body to make them look impressive. A confident pose can be far more intimidating.

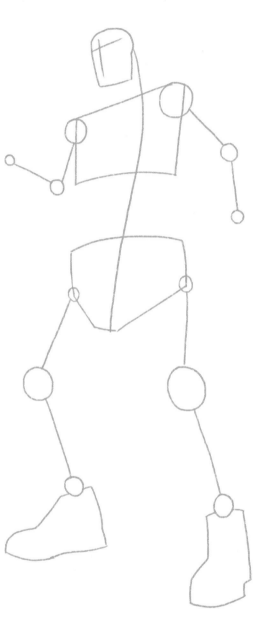

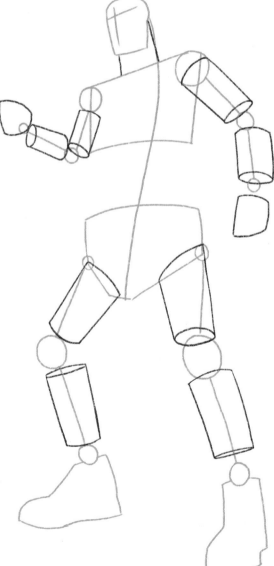

STEP 1

Draw a basic stick figure with his right arm raised from the elbow. We are looking up at this tall, imposing figure, so his legs and pelvis are large in comparison to his upper body and his eyeline is higher than normal.

STEP 2

Use cylinder shapes to bulk out your character's arms and legs, then draw the lines marking his neck and the basic shapes for his hands.

STEP 3

Draw in the muscles in his arms, legs and torso. Add his basic facial features – he has a craggy face and a cleft chin. Draw the fingers of his clenched fists.

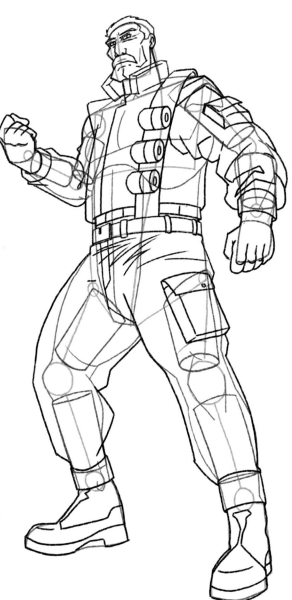

STEP 4

Give your character some hair and a mustache, then add detail to his facial features. Draw his clothes, his belt, and the shoulder strap holding his ammunition.

STEP 5

Use your lining pen to go over the lines that will be visible in the finished drawing and erase any pencil lines. Put the finishing touches to his clothes and accessories.

STEP 6

Loose material is also a feature of this character's clothing. You will have to pay close attention to the shadowing and highlighting at the next stage to bring out the folds.

STEP 7

Use shading to give depth to your character, bearing in mind the direction of the light when you are drawing the shadows.

● ARTIST'S TIP

This drawing shows that our army general is a leader. Not only is the pose slightly threatening but the perspective is from below so you are literally looking up to him.

COWBOY

How about setting a manga adventure in the Wild West? You will need a cool, calm hero to save the townsfolk from the bad guys. This cowboy gunslinger looks like he might be the man for the job . . . .

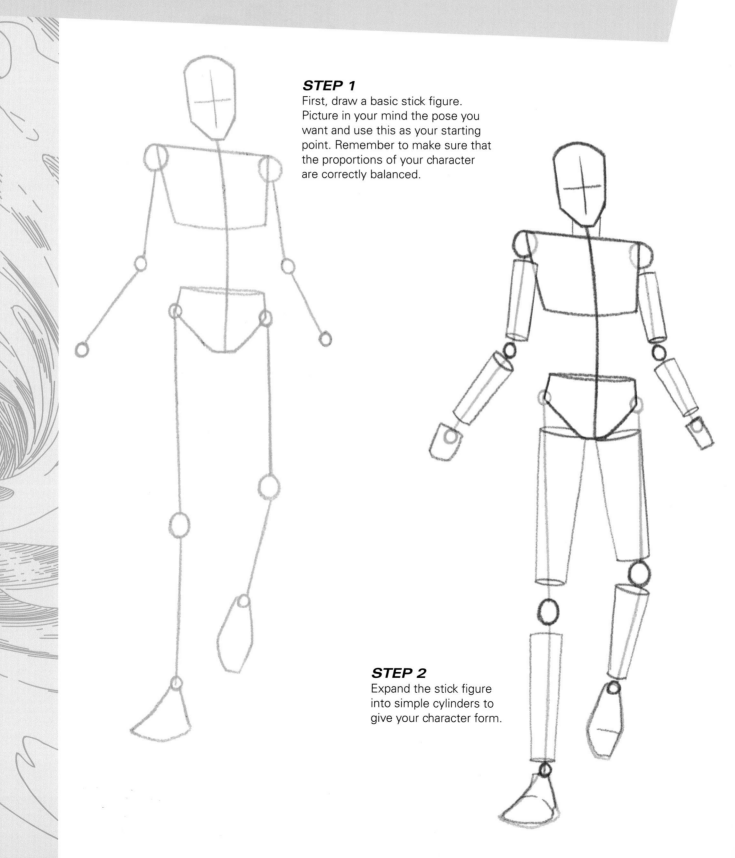

STEP 1

First, draw a basic stick figure. Picture in your mind the pose you want and use this as your starting point. Remember to make sure that the proportions of your character are correctly balanced.

STEP 2

Expand the stick figure into simple cylinders to give your character form.

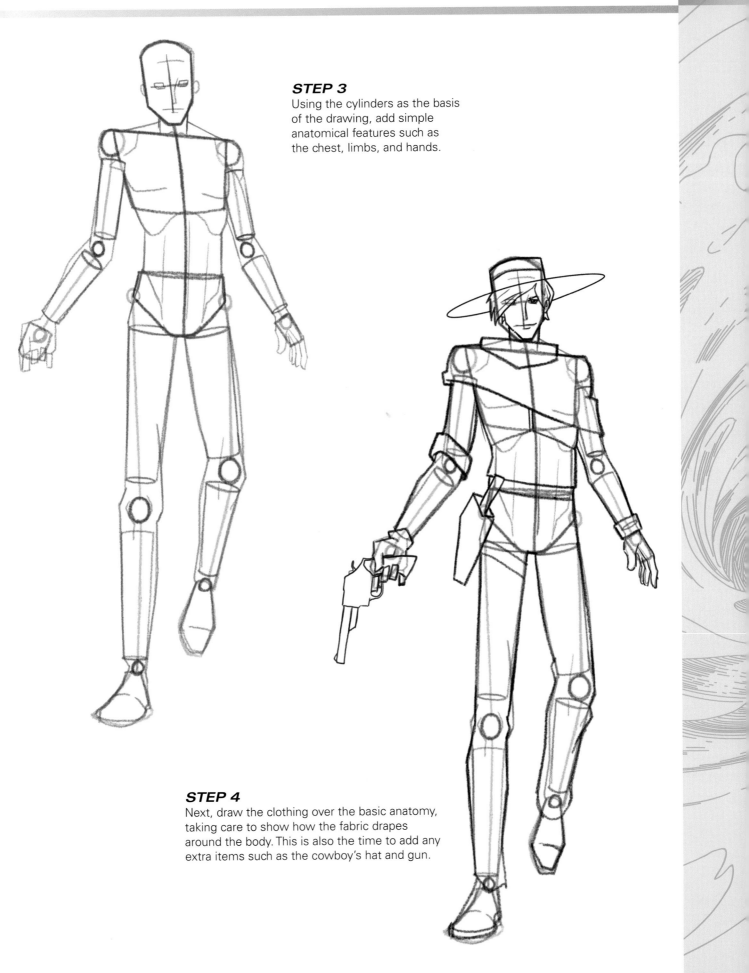

STEP 3
Using the cylinders as the basis of the drawing, add simple anatomical features such as the chest, limbs, and hands.

STEP 4
Next, draw the clothing over the basic anatomy, taking care to show how the fabric drapes around the body. This is also the time to add any extra items such as the cowboy's hat and gun.

STEP 5
With your lining pen, put in the details that are to be visible in the finished drawing. Don't line your basic stick figure or the construction cylinders you used to build the figure.

STEP 6
Choosing lighter shades, complete the coloring of your character and finish off his hair and hat. Using more muted colors for his clothing will help to create texture.

ARTIST'S TIP

The picture below shows only the shading. The light source is coming from above and to the left. Notice how the shading is heavier furthest away from the light source.

Light source

STEP 7

Use your shading pens to add depth to your figure, bearing in mind the angle of light you have chosen and making the shadows consistent with this.

ADDING EXCITEMENT

The easiest way to add movement and excitement to your images is to use focus lines. These appear much more often in manga than in Western-influenced comic artwork. Used well, they are an important part of the manga artist's storytelling toolkit.

Adding drama

If you want to draw attention to the actions or emotions of a character, an effective way to do this is to add focus lines – straight lines of varying widths radiating out from a single point.

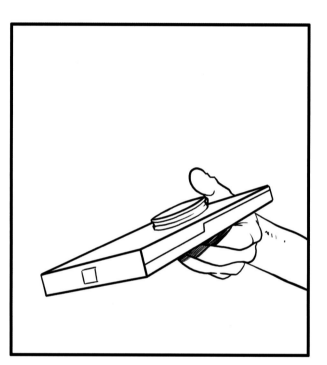

In the two examples here, the top picture shows someone holding a control button of some type. The image to the left is the same, but has the addition of focus lines. This immediately adds drama to the scene and makes the button seem much more important. Perhaps the character is about to press it and set off something devastating.

Focus lines can be used to show a wide range of emotions. They draw the reader's eye to the character's reaction and make it seem more important.

These panels show a character with a box he has just found. See how much more surprised he seems by the contents with focus lines added.

Drawing focus lines

Focus lines are simple to draw and work best as a starburst-type effect. The center of the starburst is the part of the image you want to draw attention to. Here are some examples of focus starbursts.

● ARTIST'S TIP

Try experimenting with different focus lines. Place a sheet of tracing paper over your original picture and draw lines of different thicknesses on it.

PIRATE

Imagination is the only thing that can limit the manga artist. Here we decided to relocate the action to the high seas. But as this is manga, there is nothing to stop our pirate setting course for a fantasy kingdom, a modern city, or even a spaceship!

STEP 1
Draw a basic stick figure with his head at a slight angle, one arm raised from the elbow, and the other arm slightly bent.

STEP 2
Use cylinder shapes to bulk out the arms, legs, and neck, and draw in the basic shapes for the hands.

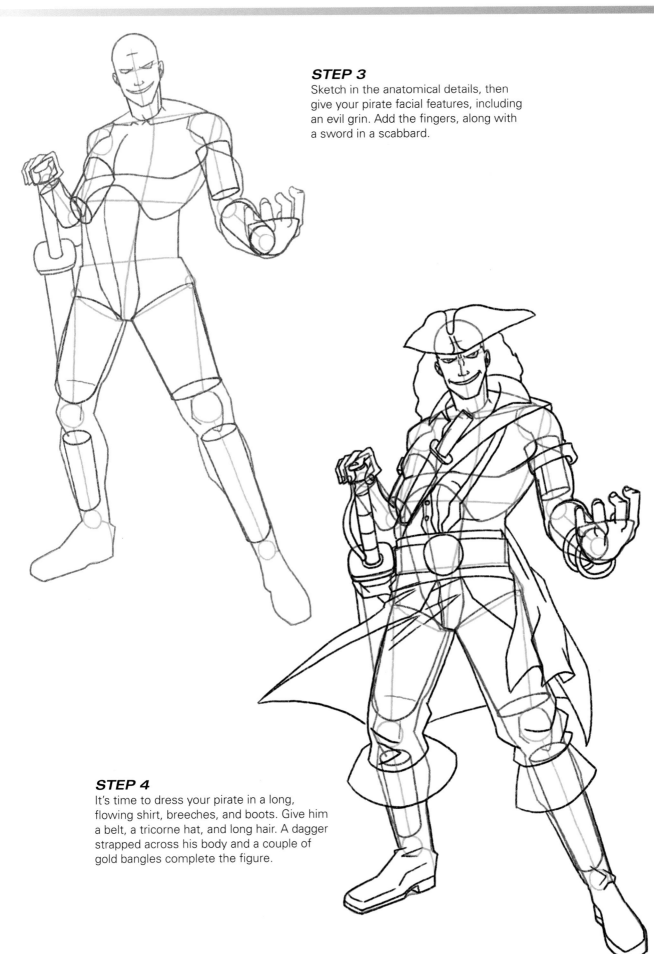

STEP 3

Sketch in the anatomical details, then give your pirate facial features, including an evil grin. Add the fingers, along with a sword in a scabbard.

STEP 4

It's time to dress your pirate in a long, flowing shirt, breeches, and boots. Give him a belt, a tricorne hat, and long hair. A dagger strapped across his body and a couple of gold bangles complete the figure.

STEP 5

Use your lining pen to go over the lines that will be visible in the finished drawing. Add shading under the pirate's chin and complete the details on his belt, clothing and weapons. Finish off his facial features and color his hair black. Erase any pencil lines.

STEP 6
Use lighter shades for the first stage of coloring.

STEP 7
Use darker colors to complete the shading, and really bring out the creases in the character's clothing.

GLOSSARY

breeches Trousers which end just below the knee.

choker A necklace which fits very closely to the neck.

cleft chin A chin with a dent at the bottom.

extraordinaire Outstanding at something.

face value The way that something appears to be, which may not be the whole story.

foreshortened To make something shorter than it really is so that a picture appears to have depth.

general The commander of an army.

gunslinger Someone who carries and uses a gun, particularly in the Wild West.

intimidating Frightening someone with a show of power.

larger-than-life Someone whose personality means they attract a lot of attention.

scabbard A cover for a sword.

starburst A pattern of lines from a central point.

T. rex A type of dinosaur, known for being a huge, dangerous predator.

tricorne A hat with three sides.

FURTHER READING

How to Draw Manga Action Figures by David Antram (Book House, 2012)

Manga Now!: How to Draw Action Figures by Keith Sparrow (Search Press Ltd, 2014)

Write and Draw Your Own Comics by Louie Stowell (Usborne, 2014)

WEBSITES

Due to the changing nature of Internet links, PowerKids Press has developed an online list of websites related to the subject of this book. This site is updated regularly. Please use this link to access the list:
www.powerkidslinks.com/um/adven

INDEX